At the
shops

D0716603

INTRODUCTION

Shopping is a big part of everyday life and almost everything we use is bought in a store. Shops vary in size – from large supermarkets to smaller corner shops – and in what they sell. Larger shops, such as department stores, stock a larger variety of different products, whereas a lot of smaller, independent shops tend to focus on one or two particular types.

Different types of shop cater for different needs, so we choose where we shop according to what we are looking for and also how much we want to spend. Even when we are not buying anything, it can be fun to browse and get ideas or inspiration.

Going to the shops can be exciting, as there are often eye-catching displays, full of colour, and you can see all the different things on offer. Shopping can also be creative, for example, when you are choosing different food items to put together to make a meal, or different pieces of clothing to make your own outfit.

Take your i-SPY book with you next time you go shopping and see how many exciting treats and more rare items you can find! You'll also get points for some things you might buy to eat, drink or use every day.

How to use your i-SPY book

As you work through this book, you will notice that the entries are arranged in groups based on where you will find things inside a shop. You need 1000 points to send off for your i-SPY certificate (see page 64) but that is not too difficult because there are masses of points in every book. Each entry has a star or circle and points value beside it. The stars represent harder to spot entries. As you make each i-SPY, write your score in the circle or star.

There are lots of different varieties of milk such as full-fat or whole milk which includes cream, semi-skimmed which only has a little cream and skimmed which has no cream. You can usually tell them apart by their different coloured lids.

CHOCOLATE MILK

Points: 10

Flavouring and colour can be added to milk for a special treat.

 Points: 15

ALMOND MILK

Almond milk is made by grinding almonds in a blender with water and removing the pulp. It is a good alternative to milk for people who avoid dairy products.

CHEDDAR CHEESE

Points: 5 ○

Cheese is created by a process involving solidifying milk. Cheddar cheese is one of the most popular varieties.

○ **Points: 10**

EDAM

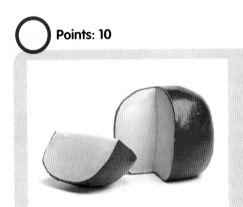

Edam is a cheese from the Netherlands encased in red wax.

Points: 10

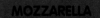
MOZZARELLA

Mozzarella is a cheese from Italy which is made from buffalo milk and often used as a topping on pizza.

MINI CHEESE

Points: 10

Miniature versions of cheese come in lots of different shapes and are a great way to try new flavours.

Points: 5

SALTED BUTTER

Butter can be salted or unsalted and cake recipes specify which type should be used. Salt is a preservative, which also means salted butter will keep for longer.

GHEE

Top Spot!   **Points: 35**

Ghee is a type of fat which is made from heating up butter. It is used in Indian cooking in recipes such as naan breads, roti and other rice based dishes such as biryani. It is also the main ingredient of many Indian sweets.

Points: 5

Yoghurt is made from milk and often flavoured with fruit.

Points: 10

Smoothies are made by blending fruit and juice until smooth. They usually contain fruits such as bananas, which make them thicker and more filling.

Points: 15

Fruit juice comes in many different varieties and is made by crushing fruit to collect the juice. Grape juice tastes sweet and can be either white or red according to the type of grape used to make it.

STICKER ON FRUIT

Points: 5

Sometimes there are stickers on fruit which say which company or country it is from.

 Points: 15

WEIGHING SCALE

Fruit and vegetables are often pre-labelled but some shops still have scales to weigh loose products.

Points: 5

GRANNY SMITH APPLE

The Granny Smith apple was named after Australian Maria Ann Smith, who cultivated it in the 19th century.

BLACKBERRY

Points: 15

The blackberry is closely related to the raspberry. Wild blackberry bushes and their fruit are known as 'brambles'.

 Points: 20

CRANBERRY

Cranberry sauce, a popular Christmas dish, is made from these small red berries.

STRAWBERRY

Points: 5

The modern variety of strawberry that we eat today was first grown in France in the middle of the 18th century. The fruits start a greenish-white, before they ripen and turn red when they are ready to be picked.

 Points: 20

BLACKCURRANT

Blackcurrants are rich in Vitamin C and a popular fruit for making jam.

GOOSEBERRY

Points: 20

These round, green fruits have a slightly striped appearance.

SATSUMA

Points: 10

Satsumas are a type of mandarin orange, originating in Japan over 700 years ago. How many other kinds of citrus fruit can you think of?

Points: 5

GRAPEFRUIT

Grapefruits can have a bitter taste and are sometimes eaten for breakfast.

WATERMELON

Points: 10

Although it can make the mouth water, a watermelon actually gets its name for the high percentage of water it contains.

Points: 15

MANGO

Mangoes were first grown in India thousands of years ago.

PINEAPPLE

Points: 10

Most of the pineapples in our shops are grown in South America. For that reason they used to be very rare and expensive.

Points: 25

DATE

Dates come from palm trees and are one of the oldest fruits known to be cultivated.

STARFRUIT

Top Spot!   **Points: 35**

When this unusual fruit is sliced, the segments are shaped like stars.

Points: 25

DRAGON FRUIT

Also known as Pitahaya, the Dragon Fruit originates in Mexico where it grows on cacti.

Points: 10

RAISIN

Did you know that raisins are dried grapes?

AVOCADO

Points: 10

In the past, the avocado was sometimes nicknamed 'alligator pear' due to its rough, dark green surface.

Points: 5

TOMATO

They are usually red, but tomatoes can come in purple, green and yellow varieties too.

ICEBERG LETTUCE

Points: 5

The crunchy texture of iceberg lettuce makes it a popular topping for burgers. More than 90% of the lettuce is water, so it contains very few calories.

Points: 5

CUCUMBER

Cucumbers originated in India and grow on a vine.

JALAPENO

Points: 15

This hot pepper originates from Mexico but is now grown in other countries too.

Points: 10

CELERY

Celery can be eaten as a snack, but is also used as a flavouring alongside onions and peppers.

AUBERGINE

Points: 10

Easily spotted by their purple colour, they are a good source of vitamins and potassium. Aubergines are the main ingredient in the popular dish, Moussaka.

Points: 5

POTATO

Potatoes come in different varieties. Some are better for boiling while others are better for baking.

GARLIC BULB

Points: 5

It's a popular myth that garlic wards off vampires. That might be a myth, but most people definitely believe that it is good for your health in other ways.

Points: 5

ONION

In the Middle Ages, onions were traded as a form of currency.

FRESH HERBS

Points: 10

There are usually many different types of fresh herbs available in our shops, including rosemary, mint, sage and parsley.

CARROT

Points: 5

Carrots contain vitamin A, which is essential in preventing night blindness. The popular myth that carrots can help you see in complete darkness dates back to the Second World War, when it was claimed carrots gave pilots their exceptional night vision.

Points: 15

PEA POD

Peapods protect small peas inside, but the whole pod is edible.

BRUSSEL SPROUT

Points: 10

There are more than 110 varieties of sprouts.

Points: 10

PARSNIP

The parsnip is a root vegetable closely related to the carrot.

Points: 5

AISLE SIGN

Look up! In large supermarkets, signs above aisles help shoppers find what they're looking for.

SELF-CHECKOUT

Points: 5

Many shops have self-checkouts to let shoppers with fewer items scan their own items.

CONVEYOR BELT

Points: 5

The conveyor belt was invented in the 19th century to speed up manufacturing. See if you can also spot the dividers used to separate different people's shopping.

Points: 5

LASER SCANNER

Modern shops use laser scanners to process bar codes on products.

HAND-HELD SCANNER

Points: 10

For more awkward items, shop assistants may use hand-held scanners to ring up items.

SHELVES BEING STACKED

Points: 15

Workers keep shelves stocked with products from the storage area.

Points: 5

RECEIPT

Sometimes receipts show extra information, like special offers for next time.

Points: 15

RIDE

The first coin-operated ride was a mechanical horse.

BAG FOR LIFE

Points: 5

Reusable bags made of thicker plastic have been introduced to help the environment.

INSTANT NOODLES

Points: 10

Adding water to dried noodles makes them expand and soften.

Points: 5

SPAGHETTI

Spaghetti is the plural form of the word spaghetto, which means one strand.

RICE

Points: 5

Rice originates from Asia and is grown in wet fields called paddies.

25

Points: 5

FLOUR

Flour is made from finely ground grains, most commonly wheat.

BAKING CASES

Points: 15

Baking cases hold cake mixture until it forms into a solid shape in the oven.

Points: 15

SPRINKLES

Sprinkles are often called 'hundreds and thousands'. They are tiny little sugar strands that can be found decorating cakes or 'sprinkled' on ice cream.

FOOD COLOURING

Points: 15

As well as being used at home for baking, in things like icing for cakes, colouring is also in lots of other foods we eat.

Points: 15

VANILLA ESSENCE

Vanilla essence comes from vanilla pods and is used to flavour food, making it sweeter.

Points: 10

TREACLE

Treacle is made from refined sugar. Golden syrup is a sweeter, pale variety and black treacle is stronger and slightly bitter.

SUGAR

Points: 5

Sugar is made from the sugar cane crop, which is a tall plant with green stalks.

Points: 5

SALT

The most common type of salt found in shops is table salt. It is made up of lots of tiny white crystals and can be used to flavour foods during or after cooking.

VINEGAR

Points: 5

The word vinegar originates from the French words for 'wine' and 'sour'. Vinegar is a popular addition to fish and chips.

Points: 10

SOY SAUCE

Soy sauce is one of the world's oldest sauces, originating in China over 2,000 years ago. It is made from soya beans and is still used in many Chinese recipes today.

TOMATO KETCHUP

Points: 5

Tomato ketchup is made by adding salt, sugar and vinegar to crushed tomatoes. Along with mayonnaise, it is one of the most popular condiments in the UK.

Points: 35 **Top Spot!**

WASABI

Wasabi is a spicy Japanese paste added to sushi. A small amount can make your eyes water!

STAR ANISE

Points: 25

Star anise is a spice that usually comes in little packets. It is used in cooking and has a flavour similar to liquorice. It is grown in China, India and many other Asian countries.

MARMALADE

Points: 5

Marmalade sandwiches are the favourite food of character Paddington Bear.

Points: 5

STRAWBERRY JAM

Strawberry jam is made by boiling strawberries, sugar and a gelling agent called pectin.

LEMON CURD

Points: 10

Lemon curd is a creamy spread with a strong lemon taste. It is used in desserts such as lemon meringue pie.

Points: 5

CHOCOLATE SPREAD

Sometimes chocolate spread also contains nuts such as hazelnuts.

LEMON JUICE

Points: 10

Bottles shaped like lemons were designed after a machine was invented to blow bottles into shapes.

TEA

Points: 5

Tea originated in China and was first brought to Europe by 16th century explorers and merchants.

Points: 10

GREEN TEA

Green tea is made from tea plants which have been processed in a different way from black tea.

COFFEE

Points: 5

Coffee plants originated in Africa and are now found in countries across the world.

Points: 10

ARTIFICIAL SWEETENER

Artificial sweeteners are a replacement for sugar in tea and coffee.

CURRY POWDER

Points: 10

Curry powder is a blend of different spices, including turmeric, chilli powder, coriander, cumin and ginger.

Points: 5

STOCK CUBES

Stock cubes add flavour to soups and stews.

TINNED PEACHES

Points: 5

Tinned peaches come either in syrup or their own juice. This is a good way to preserve the fruit, meaning it lasts much longer.

Points: 5

TOMATO SOUP

Tomatoes are fruits, not vegetables. This is because they have seeds inside them, like apples and oranges.

SPAGHETTI HOOPS

Points: 5

Spaghetti hoops are a popular topping for toast. Can you find any other pasta shapes in tins?

○ **Points: 10**

SARDINES

Even fish can be found in tins! When lots of people are in a small space, they can be referred to as 'sardines in a tin', like the little fish tightly packed into these cans.

PETITS POIS

Points: 15 ☆

Petits pois is French and it means small peas. You might find bags of frozen peas in the freezer section of the shop, but most varieties are also commonly sold in tins.

FISH COUNTER

Points: 5

The fish at the fish counter is put on ice to keep it fresh. How many different fish can you spot?

Points: 15

COD

Cod is a popular fish that is battered and fried and served in fish and chip shops. You can usually find cod in the fridge section, cut into smaller pieces, as well as whole at the fish counter.

Points: 10

SALMON

Did you know that salmon have an amazing homing ability? They return to the river they were born in to breed.

LEMON SOLE

Points: 15

Lemon sole does not taste of lemons! It is a flatfish and lives on the ocean floor.

Points: 10

PRAWN

They start off grey, but when cooked prawns turn pink. They are a common ingredient in some curries and ready meals, but are equally popular served cold in a sandwich or with dressing in a prawn cocktail.

MEAT COUNTER

Points: 5

The main types of meat you will find on the meat counter are beef, lamb, pork, chicken and turkey.

Points: 5

MINCED BEEF

Long strands of minced beef are created by putting bigger cuts through a mincing machine. The resulting minced beef is used in many popular dishes such as chilli con carne, bolognese or cottage pie.

Points: 5

STEAK

Different types of steak come from different parts of an animal's body.

TURKEY LEGS

Points: 10

Turkey and chicken legs are often called drumsticks because of their shape.

 Points: 25

KANGAROO

Alongside popular meats, some butcher sections offer more unusual options. You might also spot things like ostrich or wild boar!

SLICED BREAD

Points: 5

In many shops the baker will offer to slice the bread to your preferred thickness using a machine.

Points: 10

WRAPS

Wraps are made of flat bread and can be rolled around a filling to make a kind of sandwich. These are also known as tortillas.

Points: 10

CROISSANT

Croissants are usually crescent-shaped and are made from butter and dough. It gives them a light and crispy texture.

BAGUETTE

Points: 5

Baguettes are sometimes called 'French sticks', as they are traditionally from France. The French word 'baguette' means 'wand' or 'stick'.

Points: 10

MUFFINS

Several different types of bakery product claim the name 'muffin', but the kind you are most likely to find in your shop is the one that is like a large cupcake, usually filled with chocolate chips or fruit, and with a crispy top.

LOLLIPOP

Points: 5

Lollipops come in many different shapes and sizes and are usually fruit flavoured.

Points: 5

CHEWING GUM

The most common flavour is mint, but keep your eyes open and you'll also see fruity or liquorice gum too.

CHOCOLATE BAR

Points: 5

Chocolate is a treat for most people and comes in a huge range of varieties. Usually the darker the chocolate, the more cocoa it contains.

Points: 10

MINI SAUSAGE ROLLS

Miniature versions of full-sized foods are popular at buffets and parties.

PIZZA

Points: 5

Pepperoni is the most popular pizza topping in the UK.

FROZEN VEGETABLES

Points: 5

Freezing vegetables is a convenient way to keep them fresh for longer.

Points: 10

FROZEN BERRIES

A bag of mixed frozen berries usually contains strawberries, raspberries and blueberries.

Points: 5

MICROWAVABLE CHIPS

Microwavable chips come in individual portions for easy cooking.

YORKSHIRE PUDDINGS

Points: 10

Yorkshire puddings are made from batter consisting of eggs, flour and milk.

ICE CREAM

Points: 5

Vanilla, chocolate and strawberry are the most popular ice cream flavours. What's your favourite?

Points: 10

BAGGED ICE

Bagged ice is a convenient way to get ice cubes for parties.

Points: 5

T-SHIRT

They get their name because of their distinctive T shape.

SLIPPERS

Points: 10

Slippers are comfortable shoes that you wear indoors.

Points: 15

LEATHER GLOVES

Leather gloves were first invented to be worn when driving for a better grip on the steering wheel.

HAT

Points: 5

In a larger supermarket or clothes shop, you will probably come across a wide variety of hats, from caps and sunhats to thick woolly ones like this one. A milliner is the traditional name for a person who makes hats.

Points: 10

CHANGING ROOM

Changing rooms allow you to try on clothes before you buy them.

Points: 25

FABRIC DYE

Dye can be used to colour lots of textiles, including clothes. For example, tie-dye is a technique using dye and elastic bands on material to make a pattern.

CLOTHES PEG

Points: 10

Pegs are used to hang clothes and other fabrics, usually for drying. They can be made of wood or plastic.

Points: 15

SEWING KIT

Sewing kits are handy for fixing small holes or adding buttons to clothes.

PLASTERS

Points: 5

Plasters cover up and protect cuts from infection. They were invented in 1920 in America, where they are usually called band-aids.

Points: 5

SPONGE

Sponge can be natural or man-made. Natural sponge is found in the sea.

Points: 5

TOOTHBRUSH

Brushing your teeth twice a day helps protect against plaque and decay.

BUBBLE BATH

Points: 5

The bubbles in your bubble bath are formed from soapy water encasing air.

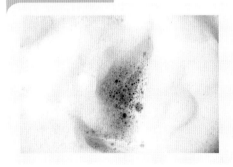

TIN FOIL

Points: 10

Tin foil used to be made from tin but is now made from aluminium.

Points: 10

RUBBER GLOVES

Rubber gloves have been worn in the home since the 1960s for cleaning and washing up, as they protect your hands from the chemicals in soap products and keep them clean and dry.

BOUQUET OF FLOWERS

Points: 10

The Netherlands is the world's biggest exporter of flowers.

Points: 35   Top Spot!

SCREWDRIVER

Different types of screws require different shaped screwdrivers.

Points: 5

TELEVISION

TELEVISION

John Logie Baird demonstrated the first working television in 1926. Since then they have grown in size and picture quality.

DVD PLAYER

Points: 5

DVD stands for Digital Versatile Disc. You can buy many popular films or TV programmes on DVD to watch at your leisure.

Points: 5

CAT FOOD

Cats have very good hearing which allows them to find prey or know when a tin of cat food is being opened!

DOG BISCUITS

Points: 5

Dog biscuits are hard and dry and often in the shape of bones.

Points: 15

BIRD SEED

Bags of mixed seeds and nuts provide a healthy and popular form of bird food.

Points: 5

For most children this is by the far the best aisle in the shop.

Points: 5

BALL

You get different balls for different sports. Most professional sports have strict laws on the size and weight of the balls used.

BUILDING BLOCKS

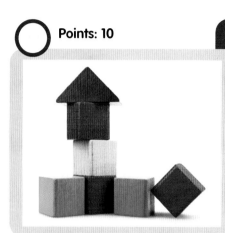

Scientists think that playing with building blocks at a young age helps children to develop problem-solving skills.

SLIME

Points: 10

Slime is soft, sticky and gooey and usually sold in plastic tubs.

DOLL

Points: 5

Dolls are thought to be the world's oldest toys: they've been found in 2000-year-old Egyptian tombs.

 Points: 5

STUFFED ANIMAL

Teddy bears are named after the former US President Theodore Roosevelt.

SKIPPING ROPE

Points: 15

Double Dutch is a skipping game in which the skipper jumps over two ropes turned in opposite directions in a criss-cross pattern.

Points: 10

BOOK

Even in the age of e-books, paper books are still very popular. Larger supermarkets usually have a small selection, but for a special title you may have to go to a traditional bookshop.

CRAYONS

Points: 10

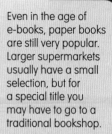

Crayons often have a paper wrapper to try and stop them from breaking. They are made from colour pigment and paraffin wax.

Points: 15

Glitter can be used to add sparkle to your pictures.

Points: 10

Glue sticks were invented to make gluing less messy and more convenient.

PIPE CLEANERS

Pipe cleaners are perhaps now best known for their use in craft projects but they were originally invented for cleaning in small holes and tight places.

INDEX

i-SPY

How to get your i-SPY certificate and badge

Let us know when you've become a super-spotter with 1000 points and we'll send you a special certificate and badge!

HERE'S WHAT TO DO!

- Ask an adult to check your score.

- Visit www.collins.co.uk/i-SPY to apply for your certificate. If you are under the age of 13 you will need a parent or guardian to do this.

- We'll send your certificate via email and you'll receive a brilliant badge through the post!